DR. PIERRE F. WALTER

BASICS OF MYTHOLOGY

Some Leading Archetypes

"Articles Series"

ISBN 978-1-468129-13-7

Contact Information Dr. Pierre F. Walter

publisher@sirius-c-publishing.com

About Dr. Pierre F. Walter

http://drpfw.info

Quotation Suggestion

Pierre F. Walter, *Basics of Feng Shui: A Beginner's Guide,* Newark: Sirius-C Media Galaxy LLC, 2011

About the Author

Pierre F. Walter is an author, international lawyer, researcher, corporate trainer, and lecturer. After finalizing studies in German Law, International Law and *European integration* with diplomas obtained in 1981 through 1983, he graduated in December 1987 at the Law Faculty of the University of Geneva as *Docteur en Droit* in international law.

The doctorate was funded by scholarships from the *Swiss Institute of Comparative Law*, Lausanne, and from the *University of Geneva*, as well as a Fulbright Travel Grant for an assistantship with Professor Louis B. Sohn at *UGA Law School Department of International Law*, Athens, Georgia, USA, in 1985. Pierre F. Walter also served as a research assistant to *Freshfields, Bruckhaus, Deringer,* Cologne, Germany in 1983 and to *Lalive Lawyers,* Geneva, in 1987.

Pierre F. Walter writes and lectures in English, German and French languages; he has written *more than ten thousand pages* embracing all literary genres, including *novels, short stories, film scripts, essays, selfhelp books, monographs* and extended *book reviews.* Also a pianist and composer, he has realized 40 CDs with *jazz, newage* and *relaxation music.*

Pierre F. Walter's professional publications span the domains *International Law, Criminal Law, Holistic Science, Psychology, Education, Shamanism, Ecology, Spirituality, Quantum Physics, Systems Theory, Natural Healing, Peace Research, Personal Growth, Selfhelp* and *Consciousness Research.* 110 Book Reviews, thirty-eight audio books and more than hundred video lectures were realized in the years 2005-2010. Besides, Pierre F. Walter is author and editor of *Great Minds Series,* which features scientists, artists and authors of genius from Leonardo to Fritjof Capra.

Pierre F. Walter publishes via his Delaware firm *Sirius-C Media Galaxy LLC* and the imprints IPUBLICA and Sirius-C Media (SCM).

For Nelson

CONTENTS

It is not difficult for the modern intellectual to concede that the symbolism of mythology has a psychological significance. Particularly after the work of the psychoanalysts, there can be little doubt, either that myths are of the nature of dream, or that dreams are symptomatic of the dynamics of the psyche. Sigmund Freud, Carl G. Jung, Wilhelm Stekel, Otto Rank, Karl Abraham, Géza Róheim, and many others have within the past few decades developed a vastly documented modern lore of dream and myth interpretation; and though the doctors differ among themselves, they are united into one great modern movement by a considerable body of common principles. With their discovery that the patterns and logic of fairy tale and myth correspond to those of dream, the long discredited chimeras of archaic man have returned dramatically to the foreground of modern consciousness.

– Joseph Campbell, *The Hero With a Thousand Faces (1973)*, p. 255.

PREFACE

What is an Archetype?

Introduction

Let me first briefly explain what an *archetype* is.

An archetype is a generic pattern or mold which exhibits certain character traits, and that typically is marked by a touch of authenticity, and that also carries a subtle energy. In modern psychology, an archetype is a bundle of elements that decisively mark a fictive character, a person, or personality, or a certain behavior.

The study of archetypes within our collective unconscious is largely the result of the pioneering work of the Swiss psychologist and psychoanalyst Carl-Gustav Jung. At his lifetime, Jung was one of the few enlightened spirits who suggested the existence of the so-called *Akashic Records* not as a museum piece of mythology, but as a real universal memory matrix of all of human experience, and he was teaching that the archetypes are an intrinsic part of that subtle universal memory surface. Jung professed that archetypes are basic to both mythology and the individual human psyche.

The origins date back as far as Plato. Jung compared archetypes to the *eîdos*, the well-known Platonic notion of 'ideas'. Plato's ideas are to be seen as primordial mental forms, imprinted in the soul before it incarnates for a human life.

In Jung's psychological framework archetypes are innate, universal prototypes for ideas and may be used to interpret observations of the human psyche; for example, a group of memories and interpretations associated with an archetype is a complex, a mother complex or father complex, which is an association with the mother or father archetype.

Jung outlined five main archetypes, the *Self* as the regulating center of the psyche and facilitator of individuation, the *Shadow*, the opposite of the ego image, often containing qualities that the ego denies but possesses nonetheless, the *Anima*, the feminine part in a man's psyche or *Animus*, the masculine image in a woman's psyche, the *Persona*, which represents how we display ourselves to the world, also called social mask.[1] Although the number of archetypes is limitless, there are particularly notable, recurring archetypal images: *The Child, The Hero, The Great Mother, The Wise, The Trickster* or *Fool*.

---

[1] See: Carl-Gustav Jung, *Archetypes of the Collective Unconscious*, in: *The Basic Writings of C.G. Jung* (1959), 358-407, *The Psychology of the Child Archetype, in: Essays on a Science of Mythology (1993)*, pp. 70-98, as well as Sally Nichols, *Jung and Tarot: An Archetypal Journey (1986)*.

The Five Primary Archetypes

To repeat it, Jung outlined five main archetypes, the *Self* as the regulating center of the psyche and facilitator of individuation, the *Shadow*, the opposite of the ego image, often containing qualities that the ego denies but possesses nonetheless, the *Anima*, the feminine part in a man's psyche or *Animus*, the masculine image in a woman's psyche, the *Persona*, which represents how we display ourselves to the world, also called social mask.

I am now going to elucidate each of these archetypes a little more in detail.

The Self

To begin negatively, I do not share the general disdain of Buddhism for the self as a concept that isolates and suffocates human creativity in an ego-bound shell. I rather sympathize with the Hindu notion of *Atman* as the Divine higher self that is considered an outflow of the universal spirit or oversoul, Brahman. It is in this sense that the Indian sage Ramana Maharshi uses the notion of *self* and this comes very close to my own idea of selfhood. However, my idea has been influenced also strongly by the psychology of Carl Gustav Jung. In Jungian psychology, the self is the archetype symbolizing the totality of the personality. It represents the striving for unity, wholeness, and integration. As such, it embraces not only the conscious but also the unconscious.

The self is not a notion that can be defined with a sunshine smile, in a positivistic drive to elucidate all and everything about the psyche. The concept of self is about as nebulous and vague as the concept of *soul*. And yet, when you explore consciousness and when you do consciousness work, and when you do healing, you encounter both on a daily basis.

Carl Gustav Jung

There is little hope of our ever being able to reach even approximate consciousness of the self, since however much we may make conscious there will always exist an indeterminate and indeterminable amount of unconscious material which belongs to the totality of the self.[2]

Jung said the self is our life's goal, 'for it is the completest expression of that fateful combination we call individuality'.[3] And it's important to see the difference between self and ego. The self comprises infinitely more than the ego. Jung put it in the formula that individuation does not shut one out from the world, but gathers the world to oneself. Thus, Jung's concept of self comes close to the Hindu notion of *atman* that, interestingly enough, is often translated as 'self'. In Ancient Egypt, this was expressed as the concept of the *Ba-soul;* the Greeks called it man's inner *daimon*; and the Romans worshiped it as man's *genius*, which was native to each individual. In more primitive societies it was frequently envisioned as a protective spirit embodied within an animal or fetish.

---

[2] C.G. Jung, *Two Essays on Analytical Psychology (1953/1972)*.

[3] Id.

The Romans believed that the *genius* was the divine force that survived after the person passed over. It was a living entity that passed from one generation to another through the head of the household. This genius spirit of the father was personified in art, which linked him with the ancestral spirit.

The Shadow

Eric Berne, when creating transactional analysis in the 1950s, was not coming up with a novelty but with a scheme that mapped insights that the more wistful part of humanity had fostered since Antiquity and that are part of all native cultures. As such, Eric Berne did a very important integrative work that has served healing and understanding of psychic processes, but that until this day never found its way to the population at large. But this ignorance is not a lack of insight or learning, but the result of systematic manipulation and suppression of intuitive knowledge through the school system in all dominator cultures.

Inner Selves are energies in our psyche that form part of our total and integral wholeness. In the ideal case, they should be balanced and in harmony with each other. This means that all inner selves should work as a sort of inner team. It is essential that all members of this inner team are fully awake and communicate with each other. In most people's psyche, however, it is as with this mystic painting that depicts the inner child as a little angel who is somnolent or asleep. The worst condition of the inner child is the *cataleptic inner child.*

While the truth about inner selves goes back to Antiquity, the insight in modern times has been made fruitful for psychiatry through Eric Berne in 1950, the founder of transactional analysis and therapy. Eric Berne recognized three essential inner selves, the *Inner Child*, *Inner Parent* and *Inner Adult*, and besides, the *Inner Controller* and the *Inner Shadow*. In my own research and auto-therapeutic work with the inner dialogue during an Erickson hypnotherapy, I encountered the presence of additional entities and found that if the *Inner Controller* is hypertrophied and thus dominating the psyche, the result is that we are unable to realize our love desires. In addition to these inner selves, I encountered an entity of superior wisdom that I called *Lux* and a shadow entity I called *Sad King* and which as the personal embodiment of my *Inner Shadow*.

The Inner Child

The *Inner Child* is an inside entity, part-personality, or psychic energy, created between our 7th and 14th year of life, and that is part of our inner triangle.[4] Positively, the inner child energy is primarily emotional and wistful, *predominantly creative*. It is the motor of every human being's creativity. Negatively, the inner child is either mute or cataleptic so that

---

[4] *Inner Triangle* is a psychoanalytic term that denotes the triangular nature of the *Inner Parent, Inner Adult* and *Inner Child*. While the inner triangle is of course a reduction of all the inner energies to just a trinity, it is important to consider it when healing trauma related to early child abuse.

its energy cannot manifest, or else its energy is turned upside-down which makes an inner child that is rebellious, capricious, willful or overbearing.

The Inner Adult

The *Inner Adult* is an inside entity, part-personality or psychic energy that represents our logical thinking, our reason, our maturity. Positively, it makes for our balanced decisions, our down-to-earth attitude and our sense for daily responsibilities. Negatively, the inner adult manifests as the intellectual nerd or through emotional frigidity, cynicism or an obsession to measure human relations on a scale of reasonableness or straightness without considering the emotional dimension and without sensitivity. The hypertrophied inner adult energy plays a major role in modern education where it results in devastating damage on the next generations' emotional integrity.

The Inner Parent

The *Inner Parent* is an inside entity, part-personality or psychic energy that represents our inner value standards, our moral attitudes, our caring for self and others, but negatively also our judging others, our I-know-better attitude or blunt interference into the lives of others without regard for their privacy. The hypertrophied inner parent energy plays a dominant role in tyrannical and persecutory societal, religious and political systems.

The Inner Dialogue

The *Inner Dialogue* is a technique that facilitates to get in touch with our *inner selves* through relaxation or self-hypnosis and subsequent dialogues with one or several of our inner selves, in a state of light trance. This state of light trance can be self-induced, a technique that I demonstrate and explain in detail in specialized publications. The inner dialogue should ideally be fixed on paper, at least in the beginning, because the voices that come up, are very soft and writing down the dialogues helps to keep focus. The technique is also called voice dialogue, for example by Stone & Stone, in their *Voice Dialogue Manual (1989)*. However, the expression could mislead novice users as the 'voices' are not really human voices, as they are not to be heard with our ears, but something like intuitions, or flashes of intuition, or sudden precisely formulated thoughts that seem to come 'from nowhere'.

Multidimensionality of the Psyche

Through the inner dialogue, I came to the insight that our psyche, every healthy psyche, is composed of a *multitude of energies or entities,* and that it is through our ego that these entities are working under a certain roof structure of conscious control. Otherwise, if this ego, for whatever reasons disappears, we enter the realm of schizophrenia, which can be, as in psychedelic trips, a welcome temporary condition.

Function of the Ego

The function of the ego is not to dominate any of our inner entities, but to *orchestrate* them, to direct them in a team-like cooperation, such as for example the conductor of an orchestra leads more than 100 musicians to play in synch in order to reproduce a musical score with accurate precision and harmonious sound. This is the function of the *healthy ego* within the multidimensional psyche. Needless to add that with most people the ego and the inner controller are hypertrophied and dominate if not suppress all other inner entities which is the explanation why such a high percentage of the world's population is completely uncreative, dull and imitative in their behavior, and why they use only about five to eight percent of their emotional intelligence potential.

The Inner Shadow

I had to explain the other psychic energies, before I can explain what the *Inner Shadow* is about. Without knowing anything about our inner psychic structure, this simply cannot be understood.

Our inner shadow is by and large a dysfunctional behavior pattern, and it has had devastating effects upon human evolution. The shadow clearly is not a creation of nature but the result of humans repressing their emotions. This led to humanity reversing the course of its evolution and entered a state of devolution.

To help you understand how the inner shadow comes about, I need to explain what *repression* means. Repression is a term coined by Sigmund Freud that describes a function of the psyche in the case consciousness meets a desire that is strongly prohibited by the inner controller. What happens in this case is that the psyche will repress the desire into the unconscious in order to uphold the functioning of the ego which would otherwise be disturbed in maintaining the integrity of the psyche.

On the starting point of repression is *denial*. All repression starts with a denial, the denial of one of our inner entities or energies, as they are part of our inner selves, or the denial or an emotion, of a desire, of a dream, of a way of realizing oneself. Denial is mainly the result of *moralism*, the quite arbitrary and culturally conditioned split between good and bad emotions, good and bad feelings, good and bad desires, good and bad behavior.

It has to be seen that *regression*, while a familiar term in cognitive psychology, is entangled with *repression*. Every form of repression results in regression. Let me explain. When I repress my sexual desire for copulating with adult women, for whatever reason, I will regress in my sexual maturity, and the result is that I will turn back on the wheel of sexual evolution, and enter the realm of *sexual paraphilias*. In most cases, I will not be consciously aware of the fact that a repression takes place, or that I deny my desire. I will not be aware that I block my emotional flow, and that I am in a fear-condition.

Please note that regression in psychology is not usually linked to repression. While repression always leads to regression, regression can also occur independently of repression, and then we talk about an entirely different set of phenomena. Regression in psychology and in natural healing typically is the fact of leading the patient back to the original wounding as from a point of effectiveness and natural psychosomatic dynamics, without the encountering of the original wounding in the dream, hypnotic or trance state, a real and full healing can generally not be accomplished.[5]

This results in the bioenergy that feeds this desire to retrograde and change polarity. I have adopted the term *retrogradation* from astronomy and astrology, and was inspired insofar by the humanistic astrologer Dane Rudhyar as it is really a lucid metaphor: retrogradation means that the energy of the planet becomes introvert for the time of the retrogradation. And the similarity to psychological retrogradation is striking!

When a child's primary biogenic vitality is impaired by moralistic education, the child looses spontaneity and becomes shy and introvert, thereby dramatically reducing communication strings with the outside world, and at the

---

[5] See for example, Villoldo & Krippner, *Healing States (1987)*, for an illustration of this principle, and for a practical example, as well as further references.

same time begins to communicate more strongly on the inside level. This becomes then, what is called a *hypersensitive child*. This leads to timidity and can result in an impaired communication ability for life, such as stuttering or extensive sweating when being around people. In the extreme case, and under conditions that amplify the original retrogradation of the natural drive for full emonic satisfaction, *sadism* begins to develop and can become an obsession that dominates the whole sexual life of the person.

Another consequence that repression brings about, is regression, which means a devolution of consciousness, a backward development in terms of psychosexual maturity – a state that is undesirable socially, because it involves a lessening of emotional and erotic self-consciousness. The insight about this process helps us to accept all of our desires and to find constructive solutions to live them out with consenting partners whatever their age.

This leads to the positive result that *desires will not regress and instead develop into higher energetic manifestations* that help the whole personality in its evolution.

A further result of repression and denial is *projection*. Projection is a psychic automatism that is a by-product of repression. When an emotion or desire gets repressed, projection sets in and what is blinded out from wake consciousness is projected upon others - who then get the blame for what is originally a part of the person's own life. This is the true meaning of Matthew 7:1-5 which says:

Matthew 7:1-5

Judge not, that you be not judged. 2 For with the judgment you pronounce you will be judged, and with the measure you use it will be measured to you. 3 Why do you see the speck that is in your brother's eye, but do not notice the log that is in your own eye? 4 Or how can you say to your brother, 'Let me take the speck out of your eye,' when there is the log in your own eye? 5 You hypocrite, first take the log out of your own eye, and then you will see clearly to take the speck out of your brother's eye.

In most cases, the inner shadow is at the basis of a person's sexuality turning into one or the other form of *sadism*, for example *sadomasochism* or *sadistic pedophilia*, which in turn often is at the basis of child rape and killing.

Sadism is a *blockage of the natural emotional flow* through a predominantly moralistic or puritanical education, often accompanied by physical punishment, which leads to a repression of the natural streaming of the hot and melting sexual energy and as a result, to *demonic emotions*, and violence, because the naturally deep sexual discharge becomes shallow or even is inhibited. As a result, the naturally hot and tender sexual feelings are disintegrated and distorted into a *compulsion for sex targeting at strong explosive sexual discharge*, as a matter of abreacting an urge, instead of embracing a mate.[6]

Sexual discharge in fact temporarily alleviates the fear armor but tends to entangle the person, who is unconscious of the affliction, long-term in sexual aggression, assault and

---

[6] See my audio books *Emonics (2010)* and *Emotional Flow (2010)* and my *Idiot Guide to Emotions (2010)*.

generally a bullying, racketing or abasing behavior, that degrades and dehumanizes the mate to a passive dummy.

Sadism was badly understood before Wilhelm Reich's indepth research on the sexual orgasm revealed that the natural sexual drive is by no means aggressive or compulsive, but controlled by empathy and love for the sexual mate. Only in sadism, which is a distortion of the natural emotional and sexual setup, this empathy tends to be overridden by an overwhelming longing for egocentric, and power-ridden, satisfaction virtually on the back, and to the detriment, of the sexual mate. This is why long-term sexual sadism leads to a corruption of the personality, as the pattern for abuse then is laid also in a general manner, and the person tends to take advantage of others in the form of a habitual behavior structure, and thus becomes what is called an 'abuser'.

But for this to happen, the pattern must have been ingrained for long, and the person must never have gained awareness of the self-distorting pattern. This is rather the extreme case, as often people become aware of their sadistic needs and begin to become suspicious about the obvious violence of their sexual behavior, and then begin to look for a way out, and may seek out a minister, physician, psychiatrist or psychotherapist for advice and consultation.

Breaking the sadism pattern is greatly facilitated through being around babies and small children, and generally, when men are actively involved in taking care of things, of children, of trees, of gardens and flowers, or for cooking and cleaning the house. *Hence, the need for involving males in early child care.* All these tasks are getting men in touch with their *yin* side, or *anima*, thereby helping them to overcome the macho or hero spirit that is negatively conducive to building the abuse pattern as a long-term affliction and personality trait. For we have to see that sadism is not only an individual problem, but also a societal concern.

Our Western culture is largely sadistic and this sadism can be shown and demonstrated with many examples from the historian's or the psychohistorian's toolbox. Thus, sadism is a direct outflow and consequence of centuries if not millennia of moralism as a sort of emotional plague that has distorted our emosexual behavior structure.

Our value system is deeply freedom and touch hostile and this value system was built because our deep emotions are out of touch with our natural emosexual base structure. This value system is against nature because it favors violence and shuns natural sexual tenderness and respectful non-violent embrace among generations, as a prolongation of necessary and health-fostering touch among all members of society.

Anima/Animus

The notion of the *anima* first appears in print in Carl Gustav Jung's study *Psychological Types*, in 1921. Some psychology writers pretend that C.G. Jung's dichotomy of animus/anima were gender-specific archetypal structures in the collective unconscious that are *compensatory* to conscious gender identity. Some even construe from this Jungian idea something like a *contrasexual archetype*, developed out of Jung's desire to conceptualize the important complementary poles in human psychological functioning.

I believe that animus/anima have nothing to do with our gender or gender impregnation, but that they are *notions related to wholeness and the dualism of polar energetic forces in us.* They are thus related to both our soul and our individual bioenergetic setup. In this sense, anima is the archetype symbolizing the unconscious female component of the male psyche and it embraces tendencies or qualities often associated with being 'feminine' in character or expression.

Anima is a Latin word and means something like *breath of life*, something that is animated with life or with soul. In patriarchal society it's especially important to stress the existence of anima as many men completely repress their feminine side and associated characteristics which clearly impoverishes them. The prototype, then, is the *macho* who is but interested in beer and football, who considers women and girls as 'household items' or at best pleasure dolls and who makes down knowledge and study as 'past-time for weaklings' - the result are the well-known *hit and sweat religions* that we encounter especially in Anglo-Saxon and Latino cultures and that are grouped around right-wing and neo-fascist political movements and interest groups. I simply coin it the *hero cult*.

On the level of the soul, anima is a personification of the feminine values. Venus, Persephone, Ariadne, and others are personifications of the anima archetype.

Carl Gustav Jung

Every man carries within him the eternal image of woman, not the image of this or that particular woman, but a definitive feminine image. This image is fundamentally unconscious. (...) Since this image is unconscious, it is always unconsciously projected upon the person of the beloved, and is one of the chief reasons for passionate attraction or aversion.[7]

Animus is the corresponding notion, symbolizing the unconscious male component of the female psyche and it embraces tendencies or qualities often associated with being 'masculine' in character or expression. In women, animus refers to developing the kind of assertive, capable powers often attributed primarily to men, and that are crucial for women's advancement in every male-dominated society.

There is of course also the negative animus archetype, which is embodied by the proverbial career woman who has no consideration for either males or children, and who is workaholic and dominant in character and expression.

Persona

The persona is the *social mask* or appearance one presents to the world. The term originates from the Latin *persona*, which means mask. The persona may appear in dreams under various guises. Importantly, the persona, used in this sense, is not a pose or some other intentional misrepresentation of the self to others. Rather, it is the social adaptation of the self, or the socially conditioned part of the self; as such it

---

[7] Carl-Gustav Jung, *The Development of Personality (1954).*

is not original but derived, self-construed, and may change according to situation and context.

A major task in acquiring self-knowledge is understanding the relationship between who one is and how one presents oneself to the world. Adapting to certain occasions, behaving in a manner suitable to that occasion, and knowing how best to navigate a vast multitude of situations is a necessary part of life. For this one needs to develop a healthy persona.

Optimally, this does not undermine the authenticity of the self. Its primary function is to navigate the space between the inner world of ego with its surrounding self and the outer world of values and culture. How these worlds rub up against one another is negotiated by the persona.

According to Jungian analyst Dr. Boris Matthews, the persona is a functional complex that operates as an attitude, or way of relating to, the outer world. It serves both as interface with the world and protection from the outer world, depending on life experience including how one has been accepted, wounded or rejected when one has naively presented an authentic thought, feeling, or reaction.

INTRODUCTION

A Murder Mythology

When you inquire in European mythology you become early aware that it's marked by murder and again murder. I shall not indulge in recounting senseless murder stories that some psychologists take for the blank truth, but just give a short sketch. Up to the reader to inquire further, using Wikipedia or other sources of knowledge.

I have said my last word on European murder mythology in my audio book *The Lunar Bull (2010)*, the text of which is published in my *Idiot Guide to Consciousness (2010)*, Chapter Four (The Spiritual Laws of Matriarchy). Up to the reader to check these sources out.

For all those joyful idealists who adore and worship Greek and Roman cultures, among them being many boylovers and homosexuals, I can only say that these cultures were decadent no lesser than ours. Only look at the sordid ways that Socrates was persecuted and put to death, to have one of many examples of the pretended 'liberty' and 'democracy' of ancient Greek culture! With our lauded 'worldwide democracy', it's exactly the same, it slaughters the innocent marginal lover who engages in a consenting embrace with an underage girl and empowers the greatest abusers, in the form of mafias and weapon-smuggling and drug-trading governments and their secret services to levels never before known in the entire human history.

By the way, the often-praised *boylove* was an idealist movement that was restricted to nobility, while that very nobility practiced slavery and violent warfare, the relegation of women to the wedlock, and the total lack of protection for little girls in a society that I can only name as 'totally homosexual' in all senses of the word. And that was even worse with the Romans where only the male had all the power and where females were having about the power as today within fundamentalist Islamic regimes. It is confirmed today by violence research that these factors suffice to qualify any given society as 'highly violent'.

We see currently the same trend. Our Western society is 'homosexualizing' itself with every year to come, a phenomenon that always goes along with a tightening of the laws, with draconian punishments, witch-hunts, spectacular scapegoat trials where people are virtually 'slaughtered' for the perverse indulgence of the mob, just as during the Roman Games, and a general fascism that veils the essential and basically runs on hypocrisy as the slime that snakes and snails the whole societal building.

I will not take a decadent culture that has lost any balance between *yang* and *yin* values as a dominator for our collective psyche as Carl Jung did it, while he relegated the female to the *anima* role. Joseph Campbell was more precise in this point, calling the female principle under patriarchy the 'counterplayer' in our psychic setup. *Counterplayer* sounds good and strong, and it empowers the female principle in the sense that while it's on the level of the unconscious, it contains real power.[8]

Let me explain more in detail what I mean. In a natural society, men by and large love women and women by and

---

[8] See Joseph Campbell, *Occidental Mythology (1991)*, p. 70. See also Pierre F. Walter, *Joseph Campbell and the Lunar Bull, Book Reviews (2010)*.

large love men. This doesn't exclude that there may be a small percentage of homosexuality, sadism, pedophilia, nepiophilia, zoophilia and other *paraphilias*, perhaps around 1 to 3%.[9]

Such a society will however not persecute those sexual minorities but tolerate them as the 'marginal' freaks, the harlequins, the bizarre folk, the black-and-beautiful sheep. It will by no means be violent toward them, while they may be ridiculed in public at times, without however being harmed in any way.

Now, what is the result of this integrative attitude? The result is that a social persecution of those minorities and thereby, a state of *civil war*, will not arise. Such a society can thus endure as it is overall *integrative* and *cohesive*. This is valid for most tribal cultures around the world and the early matriarchies, among them *Minoan Civilization* as perhaps the highest development of the *integrative social principle*.

Now, let us see how the picture looks like in a culture where pleasure was perverted into violence through *denial and moralism*, as for example in an early patriarchal invader tribe. In such a cultural setting, which is remote from the rules of nature, and typically is out to *control and dominate nature*, men by and large love men and women by and large love women. However, this fact is veiled behind a strong rhetoric of 'cultural garbage' in the form of *hypocrisy* that puts up moralistic

---

[9] To learn more about sexual paraphilias, please peruse Pierre F. Walter, *The Idiot Guide to Emotions (2010)* and *The Idiot Guide to Love (2010)* as well as my monographs *The Deeper Yielding (2010)* and *Energy Science and Vibrational Healing (2010)*.

rules that hide the reality of how people relate to each other on the erotic plane.

In fact, there will be large-scale *sadism* in all erotic relations. This leads to men professing to not only love but have Don Juan relations with many women to be factually homosexual and women professing to not only love but have Nymphomaniac relations with many men to be factually Lesbian. In general, this leads to a considerable percentage of *homosexuality, sadism, pedophilia, nepiophilia, zoophilia* as well as other *paraphilias*, perhaps around 10 to 30% of the society, thus about ten times higher as in natural cultures.[10]

Such a society will ruthlessly persecute those sexual minorities, and not tolerate them as 'marginal' freaks, but call them *offenders*, criminals and system enemies, of not sexual terrorists, and will try to completely annihilate them through Euthanasia laws, as they were practiced in the Nazi regime and other fascist regimes in the past. Such as system will be setup to not only harm these individuals, but to completely eradicate them through large-scale planned murder and genocide.

Now, what is the result of this disintegrative attitude? The result is that there will be large-scale social and legal persecution of those minorities and thereby, a state of *civil*

---

[10] Please note that I am speculating here. The percentage may be lower or higher, but that doesn't change the point I am making here, as I am only showing the structural connections. It would need much further research to present a verified theory, of course. By the way, I doubt that such a research is possible at all, as so much of this information is hidden and would need to be digged out from underground sources of knowledge.

war, in the long run. Such a society can thus *not* endure as it is overall *disintegrative* and *abrasive.*

Such a society will thus breed violence through its intolerance to sexual diversity, and through the persecution of those who defy the norm, and even prior to that, by the very fact of erecting a sexual norm. In fact, by nature, there are no sexual norms. This is simply so. It's the very fact that control was put over self-regulation, or culture over nature, or else conditioning over carefreeness that this state of *perversion* from the natural norm was brought about. You can also put it in the short form of neurosis and the blockage of bioenergy being considered superior to self-regulation and the streaming of the bioenergy.

Now, it is obvious that we are the latter, not the former culture, as our present society originates from the violent patriarchal tribes that massacred the Minoan and other matriarchal cultures who practiced what would call the 'intelligent principle' to erect stupidity as the norm. Let us assume that many of us understand this cultural madness and want to get back at natural sanity, okay? Then, of course, we must ask what is the way to go? Is that question easy to answer? Let us see.

Let us have a deeper look at the factors that we realistically could change and that have to do with our 'mythology of violence', so to speak. You got a glimpse what this *murder mythology* is actually based upon, so we only need to find the antidote to those ingredients.

You can make up your own theory of course, but please for a moment listen to what I have to say as somebody who researched for about twenty years on human emotions and sexuality. In my view, what we have to do is to rebuild emotional and erotic intelligence in our new generations, as a matter of an urgent social policy to prevent social and sexual violence in our next generation, for the karma is very queer. If we want to be effective, we need to take a holistic and integrative approach to human emotions and sexuality and change the pattern right at its root.

And in this endeavor, the old murder mythology cannot help us. We need to forge a new mythology, we have to restart from scratch, or we will perish. And of course, when I say we have to forge a new mythology, that means we have to change our consciousness, as these archetypes are well written into our collective unconscious, as Carl Jung found. But even though this is a huge change, we can effect it.

As Joseph Campbell has shown, the original myths, the ones that precedes the murder mythology, were not to the point violent, and they were not preaching rape and murder as 'solutions' for human problems as patriarchal mythology does. So over the course of human history such a deep change on the level of the collective unconscious has been effected already, so it can be done.

BECOMING AN INDIVIDUAL

The Journey to Self

Introduction

The *Tree of Life* is different from the Pedigree or Genea-logical Tree. To walk into your own life basically implies to *leave home*, and to make the psychological cut with the matrix. For this to happen, we have to go through a whole process of identity building that commences as early as in babyhood. Building identity is coupled with building autonomy.

Liz Greene & Juliet Sharman-Burke write in their en-lightening study *The Mythic Journey (2000)*:

Liz Greene & Juliet Sharman-Burke

There is a mysterious impulse in all of us to become ourselves - unique and defined individuals apart from the family bonds, partnerships and community life which give us a feeling of identity. But, as myth tells us, the process of becoming an individual is a hard and sometimes painful one. It involves not only a willing-ness to meet the inner and outer challenges that test our strength, but also a capacity to stand alone and endure the envy or hostility of those us who have not yet begun this journey towards selfhood. Myth pre-sents us with stories about how hard it is to leave home and what kind of dragons we must encounter and fight in our struggle towards autonomy. Not least, mythic tales also reveal the profound importance of a sense of personal purpose and meaning - perhaps the deepest mystery imbedded in our efforts to become what we truly are. We may not always recognize the degree to which we have avoided the challenge of individuality and the everyday ways in which we betray our most heartfelt values in order to feel we belong. In these spheres, myths can offer not only insight, but also the reassurance that self-development is not necessarily the same thing as selfishness. We cannot really offer to others what we have not yet developed within ourselves.[11]

Our present social and educational system makes us believe that there are standard truths for all of us, standard values, standard forms of behavior and a standardized morality framework for all of us. A natural science that was deeply alienated from spiritual truth and whose main advocate was Charles Darwin has led many to simply compare humans to the animal race and to deduct social, political and psychological conclusions from such a haphazard premise. The fact that we all got two arms and two legs does not mean that we can compare human beings with each other on a soul level. If we could, it would be easy and practical to work out standards for self-improvement and promote them worldwide in schools, universities and the media.

I do not say that this idea is nonsense per se. In the contrary, I am the first to advocate it and I do work hard for its realization. But only if the primary condition is met. This condition is that the methods taught are only pathways to guide people toward *their own inner guru*, and not to establish the ultimate Big Brother Gurus & Co. multinational.

The only wisdom you can learn is the one you have got already, that is contained in your continuum, your own inner space, your timeless soul, your potential. All wisdom, all knowledge that we can find, we knew it already before, and if we wish, we can find it again. I think we all have gone, as

---

[11] Liz Greene & Juliet Sharman-Burke, *The Mythic Journey (2000)*, p. 73.

humans, through the loss of connectedness with our true source.

From this experience of loss we keep a deep-down memory, somewhere in our collective unconscious. From this memory and the depression and loneliness that followed, we have developed a feeling of anticipation, a deep anxiety regarding the lost knowledge. This is why many of us today still reject what they call esoteric knowledge or make it down as superstition or imagination.

Life is our creation at every infinitesimal point of the lifeline. The lifeline itself has no beginning and no end and therefore is more appropriately described as the circle-of-life, or the spiral-of-life. There is no doubt about our impact upon the invisible threads out of which the web of life is woven. However, the depressed and alienated masses tend to believe that there is, if ever, only negligible individual control over life and that life is *per se* destined to be this or that way, according to some mysterious heavenly plan. In reality, there simply is no such plan. It is interesting to see to what extent this wrong presumption contributes to the dullness of the ignorant masses.

Contemplating the power of nature, of creation, how can one associate anything but *freedom* with the fundamental force from which sprang all the thousand things? This force has created unlimited freedom and power. However, humans have limited it to the tiny stupid thing that they have made out of life and that they use to call *their* life. They talk of *my* life and *your* life, as if we individually owned life, as if life could be *owned* at all. Only things can be owned but life is not a thing, but a dynamic, energetic process - a cosmic dance.

Only utter ignorance about the very roots of life could bring about the present state of affairs among us humans, this desperate dependency and passivity of humans worldwide. Of course, we are very busy imitating others and in that many people find their shallow satisfaction. It is a lack of energy, of commitment to ourselves and our individual, very specific mission that makes us comply with the baseline of living and transforms us into bad copies of ourselves.

Few people live original lives, *first-hand lives*. Compared with the masses of imitators and robots that run around on this globe, these people represent a tiny minority. And if you look close at them you find out quickly that they are always the contradictors, the ones who try to do things differently, the ones who are not easily satisfied, not easily duped into some petty mediocre thing, be it a job or a partner or a million in the lottery. Their value system is strangely different from the one most people have blindly adopted. When they were children, they were keen, very curious, sometimes excessively inquisitive, yet not out of low intention but from a deep thirst for human experience and interest in the human soul. In school, or more generally, in systems, educational, military or otherwise, they are the big or small disturbers, the ones who never fit in, the ones who won't comply with most of the rules, the ones also who spontaneously create different rules that, typically, function better than the rules they broke.

I do not say that you have to become a rule-breaker in order to get to know your original self, while rule-breaking at times *does* trigger a personal path of self-perfection. I do say, however, that in order to get in touch with your own originality, you have to become acutely aware of all the influences you are exposed to at any moment of your life. Why? Because there are influences that are beneficial for your growth and there are others that are harmful for it or that for the least are going to retard it. The art of life is all about being able to distinguish the latter influences from the former. Some authors and gurus require an inner purification before they admit that our soul can grow and develop. However, this means to put a time element in something that is beyond or outside of time.

Matters concerning the soul or our higher self are outside the time-space continuum. If we assume that growth processes on this level can only take place after going through a sort of soul graduation, we assemble events on a timeline that have no place there.

It seems smarter to admit that the very process of growing implies in itself a purification of old soul content. There is probably, without our knowing of it, a continuous process of renewal going on in the soul. In addition, it seems more effective to think in terms of evolution than in terms of purification. Purification focuses on the past, evolution on the future. If I want to ride a bicycle or a car and watch the road too closely, I am accident-prone. I ride safely if I gaze within a farther distance.

The same is true for personal evolution. Directed, voluntary progress is possible only if there is vision, and a vision that heads farther into the future than just tomorrow or next week. True vision is created by your *higher self*, after deep relaxation, by centering within and focusing upon your uniqueness. Many people, especially from the older generation, find it against the rules of good taste to focus upon themselves, to do self-improvement or generally to bestow attention on themselves. Many of them carry along deep guilt feelings from childhood, often having suffered mistreatment and neglect in their early years. As a result, they tend to block off when they are asked to take care of themselves. They may indulge in a good deal of social help for others, assist in welfare projects, or be otherwise useful to the community. More often than not, their self-neglect ends with a cancer or some other violent disease that crowns the big *sacrifice* they wanted to offer with their life!

We cannot be ultimately useful if we regard ourselves as useless. We cannot bestow loving attention upon others if we do not give it to us first. True religion, in the sense of the word, begins with taking care of self. This is not a *religion of egotism* as you may haphazardly consider it, but the only true religion. We do never know others good enough to judge their spiritual views, needs and belongings. We are all on different levels of evolution and different spheres of existence and belong to different soul groups and energy fields; and we all have had different former lives, incarnations and challenges, and we all carry different visions about our individual evolution and the evolution of our clan or race. It is this difference about our soul origins that makes us so helpless when we talk about what we call *spiritual matters*. Have you ever observed that people talk on different levels of consciousness when they discuss about what is called *spirituality?* The true lover of truth does not make a distinction between spiritual and non-spiritual matters since this distinction is artificial and without value. For the spiritually minded being, *everything is spiritual.* For the materialistically minded individual, *everything is material.* Life is a whole process and every attempt to divide it up, to section it, to dissect it into various parts is detrimental to grasping its perfume.

ADAM & EVE

Leaving Paradise

Metaphorically, we can compare symbiosis with paradise. Adam and Eve had to leave paradise - why? They had to leave paradise for developing their individuality, their autonomy. Paradises are not different from other things in that they, too, have a shadow: positively, they give us the almost complete illusion of security and satisfy all possible desires. But negatively, they are true prisons.

The tree of knowledge was forbidden in paradise to Adam and Eve – and we must add, *even* in paradise! Or, more clearly put, it was forbidden to them *because* they lived in paradise. To live with their full potential, Adam and Eve had to follow the wisdom of the serpent. Eating the apple, they knew each other as man and woman: they got to know about their sexual identity. It was also their discovery of sexuality since the Bible uses the old expression to 'know another' for sexual intercourse.

Through the fact of knowing the other, recognizing the sexual identity of the partner, we get information about our own sexual identity. This is an important truth: love leads to self-knowledge and is a part of our growth process. Without loving others, and I dare to specify, *making love with others*, we will hardly get to know ourselves. Through love we grow, we mature. Leaving paradise is exactly this, leaving the childhood of dependency implying a self-sufficient, narcissistic way of being, and opening up to *true relationship* where every partner is a whole autonomous beings. Love means relating and taking responsibility for one's love choices.

All sentient beings have to leave the nest of paradise. The fetus, decided he to stay in the womb to avoid the trauma of birth, would die right there! Adam and Eve, leaving paradise, survived! Their leaving paradise was a birth, a birth to life on earth, life in a body of flesh, created by desire, an *incarnated* life.

The family tree and the phylogenetic tree both symbolize the nest, the matrix. They are the symbols for the hereditary roots of the person. But they are also prisons and graves for the individual. This truth is pointed out in many religious scriptures and Ramana Maharshi expresses it in the formula that we have to go *beyond the confusion that we are the body*, that we should set aside our unconscious or conscious identification with the body. Once we have found that we are spiritual beings, sparkles of light in a universe of light or planets or stars, as the natives say, we understand that the family is only the nest and as such a kind of springboard which should catapult us into life, into our own life.

GURU & DISCIPLE

The Learning Relation

The true meaning of the guru-disciple relation is often hidden, and in our times, it is often profoundly misunderstood. To begin with, such a relationship has nothing to do with the famous American coach Anthony Robbins sells as 'modeling', that is to more or less clone another person who is very successful, in order to become oneself successful. It is by no means by cloning the guru that one becomes connected with one's own self. It is rather as it is said in Zen that one has to kill the Buddha in order to become the Buddha.

The role of some people we meet in life is to help us detaching from alienating fusion, so that we can build true autonomy. These people who catalyze in us our true desire or mission are healers, therapists or wistful lay persons who help us get free through their love and devotion, their unselfish understanding and friendship. Often these people went themselves through the problems involved in fusion and have therefore sharpened their awareness. They may have come to the insight that true love is something different from pseudo-symbiotic attachment to others and that love gives freedom, not attachment. Some of these people have little awareness of their role as healers and appear to us in humble appearance or situation, which however does by no means affect the light they bring us.

Inner freedom begins with finding out what we really want, what, in the depth of our heart, we desire to realize, and what is our life's mission. Self-knowledge is the door to inner freedom in that it gives us the tools that lead us out of our labyrinths of pseudo-symbiosis. Without knowing who we are we let ourselves over to being guided by others. Such entanglement in the energies outside of the self leads, especially in the spiritual realm, to more or less complete alienation from our own potential of light, riches and abundance.

Self-knowledge opens the door to the treasures of our own light and our own truth which is available to all of us as spiritual beings. But this treasure is in our heart and, with many of us, unfortunately too well protected and therefore buried there. Self-knowledge is a continuous process of self-exploration. It gradually unveils all the secrets of our being and our individuality that will remain untouched by collective religious undertakings.

Self-knowledge leads to comprehending the *relativity of truth* and the incapacity of man to grasp an absolute concept of truth. This limitation of the human existence is inherent in every truth. *Therefore, on the human level all that is objective becomes subjective, because subjectively related!*

There are gurus who reject worldly power while at the same time exerting a much greater power over their followers than the worldly approach would allow. Such opinions are not only not true, they are not only not spiritual, they represent what power is perceived of by most people, namely a strange, alienating and dominating force that we either reject or eagerly want to acquire.

That is why most people live in an almost paranoid contradiction; while they reject power, they are not aware that they reject their own soul power as well. Doing this, they throw out the baby with the bathwater. And while they want to acquire outside power by all means, they are not aware of the power they possess inside and which, striving for mere outside power, they diminish or smash by non-attention. The result of this strange situation is that both the power-rejecters and the power-seekers are blind to the necessity and the value of power!

The distorted image of their own power potential makes them split the human race into the oppressed or power-rejecters, on one hand, and the oppressors or the power-seekers, on the other. They tend to argue that in life there is only one essential choice to be made: to choose if you want to situate yourself among the oppressed, or losers, rather than switching to the side of the oppressors, or winners. *Tertium non datur.*

Many people unconsciously harbor this kind of an inner program, that is written in the language of either-or options. If I do not want to be poor, I have to become rich. If I do not want to be among the losers, I have to go for becoming a winner. And so on. The blind spot of these philosophies is obviously that they exclude the *tertium*, the third alternative. In general, when analyzing people with either-or philosophies, we see that they are torn up by fears, that they are rather defensive and that their self-esteem is quite low. If somebody else, a friend for example, tries to put the finger on the wound and tells them about their bias, they react either with aggression or call the friend naive, or else jovially point out that 'unfortunately the world is essentially bad' or 'people are essentially bad' and that therefore one had to make sure to find a place in the sun, cost it what it costs.

Now, if we see this clearly, we can approach the problem from a psychological point of view. This allows us to gain insight in the human nature by discarding out quick judgments about what we think or believe human beings are like. That kind of general judgments are conditioned by our past experiences and hurts. They are highly subjective. True knowledge about the human nature is not abstract and hardly to be gathered other than by passive self-observation. When we observe the phenomenon of power or what we think it is, both at the outside and inside level, we see that there is something we could identify as *soul power*, and something we could call *worldly power*. Worldly power always is a projection, while soul power is the true power.

What does this mean in detail? Let's go slowly into this, because it is a very complex matter. The danger in this kind of analysis is to jump to conclusions that are conditioned by the past, and by our old convictions and ideas. To approach the problem with a fresh mind means that we try to change our point of departure; it is like changing the observer, to use the terminology of quantum physics. This implies that we once again look inside of ourselves in order to see what power really is or how we usually perceive it. If I do this now, supposing that you do it with me, what do I see? I see that with all that I want, with all my desire for fulfillment, for accomplishment, for recognition, for outside riches, I want essentially three things:

▸   Live my life without fear;

▸   Live in peace with the world;

▸   Realize love and happiness in my relationships.

When I see now that this is what I really want, what then? Would I not inquire why I experience fear at all? And would I not be astonished why I want to live in peace? Peace - for what? I can't buy anything for that. And why should I realize love and happiness in my relationships? What value has that? Once I have the position that gives me power, once I have the partner that really fulfills me, once I have the car I ever dreamt of and the house that gives me enough space and freedom to feel *at home* - would I not feel satisfied and happy? Why should I question this damn concept of power at all?

Of course, you can refuse looking at it. You are free to do so. But once in a while, these questions tend to come up anyway, if you wish or not, and a *felt sense* of what you really desire comes up as well. And then you are puzzled, because you wonder why you should desire such commonplace childish things as peace or happiness in a world that you think has no place for that.

When we look again, we may stop a moment and see that the world hardly can have a place for that, if we individually do not *give it a place.* The world is at peace. The only creation that is not is the human being. Agreed? What you get to see in our media world is disempowering for the most part. I even go as far as saying that you, in your role as a passive media and information consumer, are *per se disempowered!* And as long as you are disempowered, your perception of power is distorted.

If you look with this distorted concept inside of you, you see yourself through thick glasses, because your perception is conditioned.

Thus, by meeting the guru, we actually meet our own inner guide, metaphorically incarnated in the guru. And through the guru we do not become like the guru, but more and more ourselves. That is the magic of the guru-disciple relation when it's understood from its origins, and not in its perverted version of *global business guruism*.

In this sense, the guru may be an ordinary person in the eyes of the world, a person from your own country and even your own neighborhood; it can also be a family member, but is usually not the father, but an uncle or grandfather. The mythological content in the guru archetype is that it is *self-reflective*, and not dogmatic, sharing knowledge, not imposing knowledge.

It may be easily understood from the foregoing that gurus must have mastered their early hangups in the sense that they must be free of the need for imposing their own story upon their disciples, but are able to see the uniqueness in the disciple, and thus restrain themselves when it goes to sharing their personal story. They know that our personal stories are only the crutches that got us on our own track, and thus they know what counts in life is the *process of becoming* itself, not the becoming as a final goal that serves self-satisfaction.

To get on your own track, you do not need a guru, but it can be helpful in certain situations and especially in bifurcating situations to see oneself mirrored in the compassionate eyes of an experienced guru. It can help avoid mistakes and taking bad routes, if only that, but it anyway a transforming experience to meet even once with a person who has reached the transpersonal state of personal realization. It's a transforming experience!

CASTOR & POLLUX

The Dioskouroi

In Greek mythology the Dioskouroi, *Kastor and Polydeuces*, in Roman mythology the Gemini (Latin for twins) Castor and Pollux are the twin sons of Leda and the brothers of Helen of Troy and Clytemnestra. According to Liddell and Scott's Lexicon, *kastor* is Greek for beaver, and *poludeukeis* means very sweet.

Castor and Polydeuces are sometimes both mortal, sometimes both divine. One consistent point is that if only one of them is immortal, it is Polydeuces. In Homer's Iliad, Helen looks down from the walls of Troy and wonders why she does not see her brothers among the Achaeans. The narrator remarks that they are both already dead and buried back in their homeland of Lacedaemon, thus suggesting that at least in some early traditions, both were mortal. Their death and shared immortality offered by Zeus was material of the lost Cypria in the Epic cycle.

DAEDALUS

The Artificer

In Greek mythology, Daedalus was a most skillful artificer, or craftsman, first mentioned by Homer as the creator of a wide dancing-ground for Ariadne. He create the labyrinth in which the Minotaur was kept.

EUROPA

A Cretan Story

Europa was a Phoenician woman in Greek mythology, from whom the name of the continent Europe has ultimately been taken. The story was a Cretan story.

The name Europa occurs in the list of daughters of primordial Oceanus and Tethys, and the daughter of the earth-giant Tityas and mother of Euphemus by Poseidon, was also named Europa. The etymology of her name suggests that Europa represented a lunar cow, at least at some symbolic level.

DEMETER

And Persephone

Demeter is the Greek goddess of grain and agriculture, the pure nourisher of youth and the green earth, the health-giving cycle of life and death, and preserver of marriage and the sacred law. She is invoked as the 'bringer of seasons' in the Homeric hymn, a subtle sign that she was worshiped long before the Olympians arrived.

She and her daughter *Persephone* were the central figures of the Eleusinian Mysteries that also predated the Olympian pantheon. Persephone, daughter of the earth goddess Demeter became the queen of the underworld after her abduction by Hades.

HADES

God of the Underworld

Hades refers both to the ancient Greek underworld, the abode of Hades, and to the god of the dead himself. In Greek mythology, Hades and his brothers Zeus and Poseidon defeated the Titans and claimed rulership over the universe ruling the underworld, sky, and sea, respectively. Because of his association with the underworld, Hades is often interpreted as a grim figure. Hades was also called Pluto. In Christian theology, the term Hades refers to the abode of the dead, sheol or hell where the dead await Judgment Day either at peace or in torment.

KING AGENOR

The King of Tyre

In history and Greek mythology, Agenor was a king of Tyre. His wife was Telephassa. Some sources state that Agenor was the son of Poseidon and Libya; these accounts refer to a brother named Belus. According to other sources, he was the son of Belus and Anchinoe. Sources differ also as to Agenor's children; he is sometimes said to have been the father of Cadmus, Europa, Cilix, Phoenix, and Thasus.

KING MINOS

And the Minotaur

In Greek mythology, Minos was a legendary king of Crete, son of Zeus and Europa. After his death, Minos became a judge of the dead in Hades. The *Minoan Civilization* has been named after him. In Greek mythology, Daedalus and Icarus were sons of King Minos of Crete. Minos was challenged as king and prayed to Poseidon for help. Poseidon sent a giant white bull out of the sea. Minos planned on sacrificing the bull to Poseidon, but then decided not to. He substituted a different bull. In rage, Poseidon cursed Pasiphaë, Minos' wife, with zoophilia.

Daedalus built her a wooden cow, in which she hid. The bull mated with the wooden cow and Pasiphaë was impregnated by the bull, giving birth to a horrible monster, the Minotaur. Daedalus then built a complicated maze called the Labyrinth and Minos put the Minotaur in it. To make sure no one would ever know the secret of the Labyrinth, Minos imprisoned Daedalus and his son, Icarus, in a tower. Daedalus and Icarus flew away on wings Daedalus invented, but Icarus' wings melted because he flew too close to the sun. Icarus fell in the sea and drowned.

PASIPHAË

And the Bull

In Greek mythology, Pasiphaë was the daughter of Helios, the Sun. Like her doublet Europa, her origins were in the East, in her case at Colchis, the palace of the Sun; she was given in marriage to King Minos of Crete. With Minos, she was the mother of Ariadne, and other children. In other aspects, Pasiphaë, like her niece Medea, was a mistress of magical herbal arts in the Greek imagination.

ZEUS

King of the Gods

Zeus is the king of the gods, the ruler of Mount Olympus, and god of the sky and thunder, in Greek mythology. His symbols are the thunderbolt, bull, eagle and the oak. The son of Kronos and Rhea, he was the youngest of his siblings. He was married to Hera in most traditions, although at the oracle of Dodona his consort was Dione: according to the Iliad, he is the father of Aphrodite by Dione. Accordingly, he is known for his erotic escapades, including one pederastic relationship, with Ganymede. His trysts resulted in many famous offspring, including Athena, Apollo and Artemis, Hermes, Persephone (by Demeter), Dionysus, Perseus, Heracles, Helen, Minos, and the Muses; by Hera he is usually said to have sired Ares, Hebe and Hephaestus.

LITERATURE INDEX

Some Basics of Mythology Literature

Buxton, Richard
The Complete World of Greek Mythology
London: Thames & Hudson, 2007

Campbell, Joseph
The Hero With A Thousand Faces
Princeton: Princeton University Press, 1973
(Bollingen Series XVII)
London: Orion Books, 1999

The Power of Myth
With Bill Moyers
ed. by Sue Flowers
New York: Anchor Books, 1988

Greene, Liz
Astrology of Fate
York Beach, ME: Red Wheel/Weiser, 1986

Saturn
A New Look at an Old Devil
York Beach, ME: Red Wheel/Weiser, 1976

The Astrological Neptune and the Quest for Redemption
Boston: Red Wheel Weiser, 1996

The Mythic Journey
With Juliet Sharman-Burke
The Meaning of Myth as a Guide for Life
New York: Simon & Schuster (Fireside), 2000

Jung, Carl Gustav

Archetypes of the Collective Unconscious
in: The Basic Writings of C.G. Jung
New York: The Modern Library, 1959, 358-407

GLOSSARY

Terms Used

Akashic Records

Akashic Records is a term that describes a compendium of mystical knowledge encoded in a cosmic information field, a non-physical plane of existence. These records are described to contain all knowledge of human experience and the history of the cosmos, as well as all human emotional experiences.

They are metaphorically described as a library, universal memory surface or universal computer. Descriptions of the records assert that they are constantly updated and that they can be accessed through astral projection.

The records are said to be *impressed* on a subtle substance called *akasha* or *somniferous ether*. In Hindu mysticism, *akasha* is thought to be the primary principle of nature from which the other four natural principles, fire, air, earth, and water, are created. These five principles also represent the five senses of the human being. The records have been referred to by different names, such as the cosmic mind, the universal mind, the collective unconscious, or the collective subconscious. Some mystics claim to be able to reanimate akashic contents as if they were turning on a celestial television set. Yogis also believe that these records can be perceived in certain psychic states.

An example of one who many claimed to have successfully read the akashic records is the late American mystic Edgar Cayce. Cayce did his readings in a sleep state or trance. Other individuals who claimed to have consciously used the akashic records include Charles Webster Leadbeater, Annie Besant, Alice Bailey, Manly P. Hall, and Helena Petrovna Blavatsky.

Ervin Laszlo, in his books *Science and the Akashic Field (2004)* and *Science and the Reenchantment of the Cosmos (2005)*, brings the latest new science of the *A-Field* and its function as the source of all manifestation and interconnectedness, flowing out and in via the *quantum vacuum* (William A. Tiller) or zero-point field, which he equates with *akasha*—cosmic mind, universal consciousness, and the field that unifies all things.

Jane Roberts in her *Seth* books describes a different version of a similar idea when Seth asserts that the fundamental stuff of the universe is *ideas and consciousness*, and that an idea once conceived, exists forever. Seth argued that all ideas and knowledge are in principle accessible by direct cognition which is precisely what I call direct perception.

Direct Perception

Direct Perception is the primary mode of learning that nature applies in evolution. Direct perception is the mode the human brain uses to receive and store information in its capacity as a passively organizing system. The child learns his or her first language through direct perception, the picking-up of whole patterns, using the integrative and associative mode of the right brain. Obedience and imitation are not the appropriate means to develop the human potential; therefore civilization can only function on an outside or superficial level, but not as a motor of integrating man into a truly functional power unit that is operating on all levels at once.

The mainstream educational system has put this natural intelligent and holistic learning mode upside down in forcing children to learn with their left brain hemisphere only, cutting off the necessary mode of synthesis provided by the right brain hemisphere. This is the single major reason why the modern educational system, while it is very costly, is totally ineffective, and brings about people who are alienated from their own inner source, out of touch as they are with their innermost human potential. This also is the reason for the astonishing lack of creativity in the corporate world, that already coach and corporate trainer Edward de Bono deplored in his books.

Minoan Civilization

The ancient *Minoan Civilization* from Crete was one of the first highly developed human cultures with a natural focus on sensuality, beauty, free sexuality and a matriarchal worldview. Minoan culture can be said to have respected what Emerson called *spiritual laws*, and they had fully integrated the female in a partnership paradigm of living and shared responsibility. No slavery was practiced and no physical punishment for children in schools was given as an educational measure. The crime rate in that culture was very low. Their religion did not worship a male god but a series of goddesses and spirits of nature.

The low degree of violence in that culture was exemplary in history, yet this civilization was virtually raped and devoured by the cruel, slavery-practicing invader tribes. Riane Eisler, in her concise exposé of Minoan mores, culture and lifestyle as part of her book *The Chalice and the Blade (1995)*, speaks of Crete as *The Essential Difference* and reminds that already Plato described the Minoans as 'exceptionally peace-loving people.'

Among all the positive aspects Eisler mentions about Minoan culture, referencing many other scholars, the most striking is that this ancient culture had a well-built model of what today we call *democracy*. Still today, the health of the Cretan population and their wistful lifestyle is famed.

A recent demographic survey has shown that in Europe, the Cretan population is by far the healthiest one, and that cancer and heart disease rates are among the lowest in the world.

Among modern scholars, Terence McKenna and Riane Eisler stand out in their correct evaluation of the value of Minoan civilization and this culture's example status for modern peace research.[12]

---

[12] See, for example, Riane Eisler, *The Chalice and the Blade (1995), Sacred Pleasure (1996)* and Terence McKenna, *Food of the Gods (1992).* See also Pierre F. Walter, *Riane Eisler and the Partnership Paradigm, 110 Book Reviews (2010)* and *Terence McKenna and the Archaic Revival, 110 Book Reviews (2010).*

BIBLIOGRAPHY

Contextual Bibliography

Arntz, William & Chasse, Betsy
What the Bleep Do We Know
20th Century Fox, 2005 (DVD)

Down The Rabbit Hole Quantum Edition
20th Century Fox, 2006 (3 DVD Set)

Bleep
An der Schnittstelle von Spiritualität und Wissenschaft
Verblüffende Erkenntnisse und Anstösse zum Weiterdenken
Berlin: Vak Verlag, 2007

Arroyo, Stephen
Astrology, Karma & Transformation
The Inner Dimensions of the Birth Chart
Sebastopol, CA: CRSC Publications, 1978

Astrologie, Karma und Transformation
Die Chancen schwieriger Aspekte
Frankfurt/M: Heyne Verlag, 1998

Relationships and Life Cycles
Astrological Patterns of Personal Experience
Sebastopol, CA: CRCS Publications, 1993

Handbuch der Horoskop-Deutung
Berlin: Rowohlt, 1999

Bachelard, Gaston

The Poetics of Reverie
Translated by Daniel Russell
Boston: Beacon Press, 1971

Poetik des Raumes
Frankfurt/M: Fischer Verlag, 2001

Balter, Michael

The Goddess and the Bull
Catalhoyuk, An Archaeological Journey
to the Dawn of Civilization
New York: Free Press, 2006

Bandler, Richard

Get the Life You Want
The Secrets to Quick and Lasting Life Change
With Neuro-Linguistic Programming
Deerfield Beach, Fl: HCI, 2008

Blofeld, J.

The Book of Changes
A New Translation of the Ancient Chinese I Ching
New York: E.P. Dutton, 1965

Blum, Ralph H. & Laughan, Susan

The Healing Runes
Tools for the Recovery of Body, Mind, Heart & Soul
New York: St. Martin's Press, 1995

Bohm, David

Wholeness and the Implicate Order
London: Routledge, 2002

Die implizite Ordnung
Grundlagen eines dynamischen Holismus
München: Goldmann Wilhelm, 1989

Thought as a System
London: Routledge, 1994

Quantum Theory
London: Dover Publications, 1989

La plénitude de l'univers
Paris: Rocher, 1992

Branden, Nathaniel

How to Raise Your Self-Esteem
New York: Bantam, 1987

Die 6 Säulen des Selbstwertgefühls
Erfolgreich und zufrieden durch ein starkes Selbst
München: Piper Verlag, 2009

Butler-Bowden, Tom

50 Success Classics
Winning Wisdom for Work & Life From 50 Landmark Books
London: Nicholas Brealey Publishing, 2004

Boldt, Laurence G.

Zen and the Art of Making a Living
A Practical Guide to Creative Career Design
New York: Penguin Arkana, 1993

How to Find the Work You Love
New York: Penguin Arkana, 1996

Zen Soup
Tasty Morsels of Zen Wisdom From Great Minds East & West
New York: Penguin Arkana, 1997

The Tao of Abundance
Eight Ancient Principles For Abundant Living
New York: Penguin Arkana, 1999

Das Tao der Fülle
Vom Reichtum, der uns glücklich macht
Mittelberg: Joy Verlag, 2001

Campbell, Joseph

The Hero With A Thousand Faces
Princeton: Princeton University Press, 1973
(Bollingen Series XVII)
London: Orion Books, 1999

Der Heros in Tausend Gestalten
München: Insel Verlag, 2009

Occidental Mythology
Princeton: Princeton University Press, 1973
(Bollingen Series XVII)
New York: Penguin Arkana, 1991

The Masks of God
Oriental Mythology
New York: Penguin Arkana, 1992
Originally published 1962

Mythologie des Ostens
Die Masken Gottes Bd. 2
Basel: Sphinx Verlag, 1996

The Power of Myth
With Bill Moyers
ed. by Sue Flowers
New York: Anchor Books, 1988

Die Kraft der Mythen
Düsseldorf: Patmos Verlag, 2007

Capacchione, Lucia

The Power of Your Other Hand
North Hollywood, CA: Newcastle Publishing, 1988

Capra, Bernt Amadeus

Mindwalk
A Film for Passionate Thinkers
Based Upon Fritjof Capra's *The Turning Point*
New York: Triton Pictures, 1990

Capra, Fritjof

The Turning Point
Science, Society And The Rising Culture
New York: Simon & Schuster, 1987
Original Author Copyright, 1982

Wendezeit
Bausteine für ein neues Weltbild
München: Droemer Knaur, 2004

Le temps du changement
Science, société et nouvelle culture
Paris: Rocher, 1994

The Tao of Physics
An Exploration of the Parallels Between Modern
Physics and Eastern Mysticism
New York: Shambhala Publications, 2000
(New Edition) Originally published in 1975

Das Tao der Physik
Die Konvergenz von westlicher Wissenschaft und östlicher Philosophie
Neue und erweiterte Auflage
München: O.W. Barth bei Scherz, 2000
Ursprünglich erschienen 1975 bei Droemersche Verlagsanstalt
in Hamburg

Le tao de la physique
Paris: Sand & Tchou, 1994

The Web of Life
A New Scientific Understanding of Living Systems
New York: Doubleday, 1997

Lebensnetz
Ein neues Verständnis der lebendigen Welt
München: Scherz Verlag, 1999

The Hidden Connections
Integrating The Biological, Cognitive And Social
Dimensions Of Life Into A Science Of Sustainability
New York: Doubleday, 2002

Verborgene Zusammenhänge
München: Scherz, 2002

Steering Business Toward Sustainability
New York: United Nations University Press, 1995

Uncommon Wisdom
Conversations with Remarkable People
New York: Bantam, 1989

The Science of Leonardo
Inside the Mind of the Great Genius of the Renaissance
New York: Anchor Books, 2008
New York: Bantam Doubleday, 2007 (First Publishing)

Chopra, Deepak

Creating Affluence
The A-to-Z Steps to a Richer Life
New York: Amber-Allen Publishing (2003)

Synchrodestiny
Discover the Power of Meaningful Coincidence to Manifest Abundance
Audio Book / CD
Niles, IL: Nightingale-Conant, 2006

The Seven Spiritual Laws of Success
A Practical Guide to the Fulfillment of Your Dreams
Audio Book / CD
New York: Amber-Allen Publishing (2002)

Die Sieben Geistigen Gesetze des Erfolgs
Berlin: Ullstein Verlag, 2004

The Spontaneous Fulfillment of Desire
Harnessing the Infinite Power of Coincidence
New York: Random House Audio, 2003

Covey, Stephen R.

The 7 Habits of Highly Effective People
Powerful Lessons in Personal Change
New York: Free Press, 2004
15th Anniversary Edition
First Published in 1989

Die 7 Wege zur Effektivität
Prinzipien für persönlichen und beruflichen Erfolg
Offenbach: Gabal Verlag, 2009

The 8th Habit
From Effectiveness to Greatness
London: Simon & Schuster, 2004

Der 8. Weg
Von der Effektivität zur wahren Grösse
6. Auflage
Offenbach: Gabal Verlag, 2006

Craze, Richard

Feng Shui
Feng Shui Book & Card Pack
London: Thorsons, 1997

De Bono, Edward

The Use of Lateral Thinking
New York: Penguin, 1967

The Mechanism of Mind
New York: Penguin, 1969

Sur/Petition
London: HarperCollins, 1993

Tactics
London: HarperCollins, 1993
First published in 1985

Taktiken und Strategien erfolgreicher Menschen
Frankfurt/M: MVG Verlag, 1995

Serious Creativity
Using the Power of Lateral Thinking to Create New Ideas
London: HarperCollins, 1996

Dürckheim, Karlfried Graf

Hara: The Vital Center of Man
Rochester: Inner Traditions, 2004

Hara
Die Erdmitte des Menschen
Neuausgabe
München: O.W. Barth bei Scherz, 2005

Zen and Us
New York: Penguin Arkana 1991

The Call for the Master
New York: Penguin Books, 1993

Absolute Living
The Otherworldly in the World and the Path to Maturity
New York: Penguin Arkana, 1992

The Way of Transformation
Daily Life as a Spiritual Exercise
London: Allen & Unwin, 1988

Der Alltag als Übung
Vom Weg der Verwandlung
Bern: Huber, 2008

The Japanese Cult of Tranquility
London: Rider, 1960

Kultur der Stille
Frankfurt/M: Weltz Verlag, 1997

Eisler, Riane

The Chalice and the Blade
Our history, Our future
San Francisco: Harper & Row, 1995

Kelch und Schwert, Unsere Geschichte, unsere Zukunft
Weibliches und männliches Prinzip in der Geschichte
Freiburg: Arbor Verlag, 2005

Sacred Pleasure: Sex, Myth and the Politics of the Body
New Paths to Power and Love
San Francisco: Harper & Row, 1996

The Partnership Way
New Tools for Living and Learning
With David Loye
Brandon, VT: Holistic Education Press, 1998

The Real Wealth of Nations
Creating a Caring Economics
San Francisco: Berrett-Koehler Publishers, 2008

Emoto, Masaru

The Hidden Messages in Water
New York: Atria Books, 2004

Die Botschaft des Wassers
Burgrain: Koha Verlag, 2008

The Secret Life of Water
New York: Atria Books, 2005

Die Heilkraft des Wassers
Burgrain: Koha Verlag, 2004

Goleman, Daniel

Emotional Intelligence
New York, Bantam Books, 1995

EQ. Emotionale Intelligenz
München: DTV Verlag, 1997

Freud, Sigmund

Three Essays on the Theory of Sexuality
in: The Standard Edition of the Complete Psychological
Works of Sigmund Freud
London: Hogarth Press, 1953-54
Vol. 7, pp. 130 ff
(first published in 1905)

Drei Abhandlungen zur Sexualtheorie
Frankfurt/M: Fischer, 1991

The Interpretation of Dreams
New York: Avon, Reissue Edition, 1980
and in: The Standard Edition of the Complete Psychological
Works of Sigmund Freud , (24 Volumes) ed. by James Strachey
New York: W. W. Norton & Company, 1976

Die Traumdeutung
Frankfurt/M: Fischer, 2005

Totem and Taboo
New York: Routledge, 1999
Originally published in 1913

Totem und Tabu
Einige Übereinstimmungen im Seelenleben der Wilden und
der Neurotiker
Frankfurt/M: Fischer Verlag, 1972

Goswami, Amit

The Self-Aware Universe
How Consciousness Creates the Material World
New York: Tarcher/Putnam, 1995

Das Bewusste Universum
Wie Bewusstsein die materielle Welt erschafft
Stuttgart: Lüchow Verlag, 2007

Greene, Liz

Astrology of Fate
York Beach, ME: Red Wheel/Weiser, 1986

Saturn
A New Look at an Old Devil
York Beach, ME: Red Wheel/Weiser, 1976

The Astrological Neptune and the Quest for Redemption
Boston: Red Wheel Weiser, 1996

The Mythic Journey
With Juliet Sharman-Burke
The Meaning of Myth as a Guide for Life
New York: Simon & Schuster (Fireside), 2000

Die Mythische Reise
Die Bedeutung der Mythen als ein Führer durch das Leben
München: Atmosphären Verlag, 2004

The Mythic Tarot
With Juliet Sharman-Burke
New York: Simon & Schuster (Fireside), 2001
Originally published in 1986

Le Tarot Mythique
Une nouvelle approche du Tarot
Paris: Solar, 1988

The Luminaries

The Psychology of the Sun and Moon in the Horoscope
With Howard Sasportas
York Beach, ME: Red Wheel/Weiser, 1992

Sonne und Mond
Die Bedeutung der grossen Lichter in der Mythologie und im Horoskop
Saarbrücken: Neue Erde/Lentz, 2000

Greer, John Michael

Earth Divination, Earth Magic
A Practical Guide to Geomancy
New York: Llewellyn Publications, 1999

Hicks, Esther and Jerry

The Amazing Power of Deliberate Intent
Living the Art of Allowing
Carlsbad, CA: Hay House, 2006

Holmes, Ernst

The Science of Mind
A Philosophy, A Faith, A Way of Life
New York: Jeremy P. Tarcher/Putnam, 1998
First Published in 1938

Houston, Jean

The Possible Human
A Course in Enhancing Your Physical, Mental, and Creative Abilities
New York: Jeremy P. Tarcher/Putnam, 1982

Huang, Alfred

The Complete I Ching
The Definite Translation from Taoist Master Alfred Huang
Rochester, NY: Inner Traditions, 1998

Hunt, Valerie

Infinite Mind
Science of the Human Vibrations of Consciousness
Malibu, CA: Malibu Publishing, 2000

Huxley, Aldous

The Doors of Perception and Heaven and Hell
London: HarperCollins (Flamingo), 1994
(originally published in 1954)

The Perennial Philosophy
San Francisco: Harper & Row, 1970

Jackson, Nigel

The Rune Mysteries
With Silver RavenWolf
St. Paul, Minn.: Llewellyn Publications, 2000

Jung, Carl Gustav

Archetypen
München: DTV Verlag, 2001

Archetypes of the Collective Unconscious
in: The Basic Writings of C.G. Jung
New York: The Modern Library, 1959, 358-407

Collected Works
New York, 1959

Dialectique du moi et de l'inconscient
Paris, Gallimard, 1991

On the Nature of the Psyche
in: The Basic Writings of C.G. Jung
New York: The Modern Library, 1959, 47-133

Psychological Types
Collected Writings, Vol. 6
Princeton: Princeton University Press, 1971

Psychologie und Religion
München: DTV Verlag, 2001

Psychology and Religion
in: The Basic Writings of C.G. Jung
New York: The Modern Library, 1959, 582-655

Religious and Psychological Problems of Alchemy
in: The Basic Writings of C.G. Jung
New York: The Modern Library, 1959, 537-581

Symbol und Libido
Freiburg: Walter Verlag, 1987

Synchronizität, Akausalität und Okkultismus
Frankfurt/M: DTV, 2001

The Basic Writings of C.G. Jung
New York: The Modern Library, 1959

The Development of Personality
Collected Writings, Vol. 17
Princeton: Princeton University Press, 1954

The Meaning and Significance of Dreams
Boston: Sigo Press, 1991

The Myth of the Divine Child
in: Essays on A Science of Mythology
Princeton, N.J.: Princeton University Press Bollingen
Series XXII, 1969. (With Karl Kerenyi)

Traum und Traumdeutung
München: DTV Verlag, 2001

Two Essays on Analytical Psychology
Collected Writings, Vol. 7
Princeton: Princeton University Press, 1972
First published by Routledge & Kegan Paul, Ltd., 1953

Zur Psychologie westlicher und östlicher Religion
Fünfte Auflage
Olten: Walter Verlag, 1988

Karagulla, Shafica

The Chakras
Correlations between Medical Science and Clairvoyant Observation
With Dora van Gelder Kunz
Wheaton: Quest Books, 1989

Die Chakras und die feinstofflichen Körper des Menschen
Mit Dora van Gelder-Kunz
Grafing: Aquamarin Verlag, 1994

Kiang, Kok Kok

The I Ching
An Illustrated Guide to the Chinese Art of Divination
Singapore: Asiapac, 1993

Kingston, Karen

Creating Sacred Space With Feng Shui
New York: Broadway Books, 1997

Krishnamurti, J.

Freedom From The Known
San Francisco: Harper & Row, 1969

The First and Last Freedom
San Francisco: Harper & Row, 1975

Education and the Significance of Life
London: Victor Gollancz, 1978

Commentaries on Living
First Series
London: Victor Gollancz, 1985
Commentaries on Living
Second Series
London: Victor Gollancz, 1986

Krishnamurti's Journal
London: Victor Gollancz, 1987

Krishnamurti's Notebook
London: Victor Gollancz, 1986

Beyond Violence
London: Victor Gollancz, 1985

Beginnings of Learning
New York: Penguin, 1986

The Penguin Krishnamurti Reader
New York: Penguin, 1987

On God
San Francisco: Harper & Row, 1992

On Fear
San Francisco: Harper & Row, 1995

The Essential Krishnamurti
San Francisco: Harper & Row, 1996

The Ending of Time
With Dr. David Bohm
San Francisco: Harper & Row, 1985

Kwok, Man-Ho
The Feng Shui Kit
London: Piatkus, 1995

Lakhovsky, Georges
La Science et le Bonheur
Longévité et Immortalité par les Vibrations
Paris: Gauthier–Villars, 1930

Le Secret de la Vie
Paris: Gauthier–Villars, 1929

Secret of Life
New York: Kessinger Publishing, 2003

L'étiologie du Cancer
Paris: Gauthier–Villars, 1929

L'Universion
Paris: Gauthier–Villars, 1927

Leadbeater, Charles Webster

Astral Plane
Its Scenery, Inhabitants and Phenomena
Kessinger Publishing Reprint Edition, 1997

Dreams
What they Are and How they are Caused
London: Theosophical Publishing Society, 1903
Kessinger Publishing Reprint Edition, 1998

The Inner Life
Chicago: The Rajput Press, 1911
Kessinger Publishing

Leonard, George, Murphy, Michael

The Live We Are Given
A Long Term Program for Realizing the
Potential of Body, Mind, Heart and Soul
New York: Jeremy P. Tarcher/Putnam, 1984

Liedloff, Jean

Continuum Concept
In Search of Happiness Lost
New York: Perseus Books, 1986
First published in 1977

Auf der Suche nach dem verlorenen Glück
Gegen die Zerstörung der Glücksfähigkeit in der frühen Kindheit
München: C.H. Beck Verlag, 2006

Lip, Evelyn

The Design & Feng Shui of Logos, Trademarks and Signboards
Singapore: Prentice Hall, 1995

Long, Max *Freedom*

The Secret Science at Work
The Huna Method as a Way of Life
Marina del Rey: De Vorss Publications, 1995
Originally published in 1953

Geheimes Wissen hinter Wundern
Die Entdeckung der HUNA-Lehre
Darmstadt: Schirner Verlag, 2006

Growing Into Light
A Personal Guide to Practicing the Huna Method,
Marina del Rey: De Vorss Publications, 1955

Lowen, Alexander

Angst vor dem Leben
Über den Ursprung seelischen Leides und den Weg
zu einem reicheren Dasein
München: Goldmann Wilhelm, 1989

Bioenergetics
New York: Coward, McGoegham 1975

Bioenergetik
Therapie der Seele durch Arbeit mit dem Körper
Berlin: Rowohlt, 2008

Depression and the Body
The Biological Basis of Faith and Reality
New York: Penguin, 1992

Fear of Life
New York: Bioenergetic Press, 2003

Honoring the Body
The Autobiography of Alexander Lowen
New York: Bioenergetic Press, 2004

Joy
The Surrender to the Body and to Life
New York: Penguin, 1995

Love and Orgasm
New York: Macmillan, 1965

Love, Sex and Your Heart
New York: Bioenergetics Press, 2004

Narcissism: Denial of the True Self
New York: Macmillan, Collier Books, 1983

Narzissmus
Die Verleugnung des wahren Selbst
München: Goldmann Wilhelm, 1992

Pleasure: A Creative Approach to Life
New York: Bioenergetics Press, 2004
First published in 1970

The Language of the Body
Physical Dynamics of Character Structure
New York: Bioenergetics Press, 2006

Maharshi, Ramana

The Collected Works of Ramana Maharshi
New York: Sri Ramanasramam, 2002

The Essential Teachings of Ramana Maharshi
A Visual Journey
New York: Inner Directions Publishing, 2002
by Matthew Greenblad

Sei was du bist!
München: O.W. Barth, 2001

Nan Yar? Wer bin ich?
München: Kamphausen, 2002

Malinowski, Bronislaw

Crime und Custom in Savage Society
London: Kegan, 1926

Sex and Repression in Savage Society
London: Kegan, 1927

The Sexual Life of Savages in North West Melanesia
New York: Halycon House, 1929

Das Geschlechtsleben der Wilden in Nordwest-Melanesien
Liebe, Ehe und Familienleben bei den Eingeborenen der
Trobriand Inseln, Britisch-Neuguinea
Eschborn: Klotz Verlag, 2005

McKenna, Terence

The Archaic Revival
San Francisco: Harper & Row, 1992

Food of The Gods
A Radical History of Plants, Drugs and Human Evolution
London: Rider, 1992

Die Speisen der Götter
Berlin: Synergia/Syntropia, 1996

The Invisible Landscape
Mind Hallucinogens and the I Ching
New York: HarperCollins, 1993
(With Dennis McKenna)

True Hallucinations
Being the Account of the Author's Extraordinary
Adventures in the Devil's Paradise
New York: Fine Communications, 1998

McNiff, Shaun

Art as Medicine
Boston: Shambhala, 1992

Art as Therapy
Creating a Therapy of the Imagination
Boston/London: Shambhala, 1992

Trust the Process
An Artist's Guide to Letting Go
New York: Shambhala Publications, 1998

Miller, Mary & Taube, Karl

*An Illustrated Dictionary of the Gods and Symbols of
Ancient Mexico and the Maya*
London: Thames & Hudson, 1993

Moore, Thomas

Care of the Soul
A Guide for Cultivating Depth and Sacredness in Everyday Life
New York: Harper & Collins, 1994

Die Seele Lieben
Tiefe und Spiritualität im täglichen Leben
München: Droemer Knaur, 1995

Murphy, Joseph

The Power of Your Subconscious Mind
West Nyack, N.Y.: Parker, 1981, N.Y.: Bantam, 1982
Originally published in 1962

Die Macht Ihres Unterbewusstseins
München: Hugendubel, 2000

La puissance de votre subconscient
Genève: Ramón Keller, 1967

The Miracle of Mind Dynamics
New York: Prentice Hall, 1964

Miracle Power for Infinite Riches
West Nyack, N.Y.: Parker, 1972

The Amazing Laws of Cosmic Mind Power
West Nyack, N.Y.: Parker, 1973

Secrets of the I Ching
West Nyack, N.Y.: Parker, 1970

Think Yourself Rich
Use the Power of Your Subconscious Mind to Find True Wealth
Revised by Ian D. McMahan, Ph.D.
Paramus, NJ: Reward Books, 2001

Das Erfolgsbuch
Wie sie alles im Leben erreichen können
Hamburg: Heyne Verlag, 2002

Wahrheiten die ihr Leben verändern
Dr. Joseph Murphys Vermächtnis
München: Hugendubel, 1996

Murphy, Michael

The Future of the Body
Explorations into the Further Evolution of Human Nature
New York: Jeremy P. Tarcher/Putnam, 1992

Der Quanten-Mensch
München: Ludwig Verlag, 1996

Myers, Tony Pearce

The Soul of Creativity
Insights into the Creative Process
Novato, CA: New World Library, 1999

Narby, Jeremy

The Cosmic Serpent
DNA and the Origins of Knowledge
New York: J. P. Tarcher, 1999

Die Kosmische Schlange
Auf den Pfaden der Schamanen zu den Ursprüngen modernen Wissens
Stuttgart: Klett-Cotta, 2007

Nau, Erika

Self-Awareness Through Huna
Virginia Beach: Donning, 1981

Selbstbewusst durch Huna
Die magische Weisheit Hawaiis
2. Auflage
Basel: Sphinx Verlag, 1989

Ni, Hua-Ching

I Ching
The Book of Changes and the Unchanging Truth
2nd edition
Santa Barbara: Seven Star Communications, 1999

Esoteric Tao The Ching
The Shrine of the Eternal Breath of Tao
Santa Monica: College of Tao and Traditional
Chinese Healing, 1992

The Complete Works of Lao Tzu
Tao The Ching & Hua Hu Ching
Translation and Elucidation by Hua-Ching Ni
Santa Monica: Seven Star Communications, 1995

Nichols, Sallie

Jung and Tarot: An Archetypal Journey
New York: Red Wheel/Weiser, 1986

Die Psychologie des Tarot
Interlaken: Ansata Verlag, 1996

Ong, Hean-Tatt

Amazing Scientific Basis of Feng-Shui
Kuala Lumpur: Eastern Dragon Press, 1997

Ostrander, Sheila & Schroeder, Lynn

Superlearning 2000
New York: Delacorte Press, 1994

Superlearning
Die revolutionäre Lernmethode
München: Scherz Verlag, 1979

Supermemory
New York: Carroll & Graf, 1991

SuperMemory
Der Weg zum optimalen Gedächtnis
München: Goldmann, 1996

Radin, Dean

The Conscious Universe
The Scientific Truth of Psychic Phenomena
San Francisco: Harper & Row, 1997

Entangled Minds
Extrasensory Experiences in a Quantum Reality
New York: Paraview Pocket Books, 2006

Reich, Wilhelm

A Review of the Theories, dating from The 17th Century,
on the Origin of Organic Life, by Arthur Hahn, Literature Assistant at the
Institut für Sexualökonomische Lebensforschung, Biologisches
Laboratorium, Oslo, 1938
©1979 by Mary Boyd Higgins as Director of the Wilhelm Reich Infant
Trust (XEROX Copy from the Wilhelm Reich Museum)

CORE (Cosmic Orgone Engineering)
Part I, Space Ships, DOR and DROUGHT
©1984, Orgone Institute Press
Der Einbruch der sexuellen Zwangsmoral
Frankfurt/M: Fischer, 1981

Die Entdeckung des Orgons II
Der Krebs
Frankfurt/M: Fischer, 1981
Köln: Kiepenheuer & Witsch, 1984

Die Funktion des Orgasmus
Sexualökonomische Grundprobleme der biologischen Energie
Köln: Kiepenheuer & Witsch, 1987

Die Massenpsychologie des Faschismus
Frankfurt/M: Fischer, 1974

Die sexuelle Revolution
Frankfurt/M: Fischer, 1966

Early Writings 1
New York: Farrar, Straus & Giroux, 1975

Ether, God & Devil & Cosmic Superimposition
New York: Farrar, Straus & Giroux, 1972
Originally published in 1949

Frühe Schriften 1
Aus den Jahren 1920–1925
Frankfurt/M: Fischer, 1983

Frühe Schriften 2
Genitalität in der Theorie und Therapie der Neurose
Frankfurt/M: Fischer, 1985

Genitality in the Theory and Therapy of Neurosis
©1980 by Mary Boyd Higgins as Director
of the Wilhelm Reich Infant Trust

Leidenschaften der Jugend
Köln: Kiepenheuer & Witsch, 1984

L'irruption de la morale sexuelle
Paris: Payot, 1972

Menschen im Staat
Frankfurt/M: Nexus, 1982

People in Trouble
©1974 by Mary Boyd Higgins as Director
of the Wilhelm Reich Infant Trust

Record of a Friendship
The Correspondence of Wilhelm Reich and A. S. Neill
New York, Farrar, Straus & Giroux, 1981

Selected Writings
An Introduction to Orgonomy
New York: Farrar, Straus & Giroux, 1973

The Bioelectrical Investigation of Sexuality and Anxiety
New York: Farrar, Straus & Giroux, 1983
Originally published in 1935

The Bion Experiments
reprinted in *Selected Writings*
New York: Farrar, Straus & Giroux, 1973

The Cancer Biopathy (The Orgone, Vol. 2)
New York: Farrar, Straus & Giroux, 1973

The Function of the Orgasm (The Orgone, Vol. 1)
Orgone Institute Press, New York, 1942

The Invasion of Compulsory Sex Morality
New York: Farrar, Straus & Giroux, 1971
Originally published in 1932

The Leukemia Problem: Approach
©1951, Orgone Institute Press
Copyright Renewed 1979
XEROX Copy from the Wilhelm Reich Museum

The Mass Psychology of Fascism
New York: Farrar, Straus & Giroux, 1970
Originally published in 1933

The Orgone Energy Accumulator
Its Scientific and Medical Use
©1951, 1979, Orgone Institute Press
XEROX Copy from the Wilhelm Reich Museum

The Schizophrenic Split
©1945, 1949, 1972 by Mary Boyd Higgins as Director of the
Wilhelm Reich Infant Trust
XEROX Copy from the Wilhelm Reich Museum

The Sexual Revolution
©1945, 1962 by Mary Boyd Higgins as Director
of the Wilhelm Reich Infant Trust

Zeugnisse einer Freundschaft
Der Briefwechsel zwischen Wilhelm Reich und A.S.
Neill (1936–1957)
Köln: Kiepenheuer & Witsch, 1986

Roberts, Jane

The Nature of Personal Reality
New York: Amber-Allen Publishing, 1994
First published in 1974

Die Natur der Persönlichen Realität
Ein neues Bewusstsein als Quelle der Kreativität
München: Kailash Verlag, 2007

The Nature of the Psyche
Its Human Expression
New York, Amber-Allen Publishing, 1996
First published in 1979

Die Natur der Psyche
Ihr menschlicher Ausdruck in Kreativität, Liebe, Sexualität
Genf: Ariston Verlag, 1985

Die Natur der Psyche
Ihr menschlicher Ausdruck in Kreativität, Liebe, Sexualität
München: Kailash Verlag, 2008

Rudhyar, Dane

Astrology of Personality
A Reformulation of Astrological Concepts and Ideals in
Terms of Contemporary Psychology and Philosophy
New York: Aurora Press, 1990

An Astrological Triptych
Gifts of the Spirit, The Way Through, and The Illumined Road
New York: Aurora Press, 1991

Astrological Mandala
New York: Vintage Books, 1994

L'astrologie de la transformation
Paris: Rocher, 1984

Ruiz, Don Miguel

The Four Agreements
A Practical Guide to Personal Freedom
San Rafael, CA: Amber Allen Publishing, 1997

The Mastery of Love
A Practical Guide to the Art of Relationship
San Rafael, CA: Amber Allen Publishing, 1999

The Voice of Knowledge
A Practical Guide to Inner Peace
San Rafael, CA: Amber Allen Publishing, 2004

Ruperti, Alexander

Cycles of Becoming
The Planetary Pattern of Growth
New York: CRCS Publications, 1978

Sheldrake, Rupert

A New Science of Life
The Hypothesis of Morphic Resonance
Rochester: Park Street Press, 1995

Das Schöpferische Universum
Die Theorie des morphogenetischen Feldes
Neue und erweiterte Auflage
Berlin: Ullstein, 2009

Shone, Ronald

Creative Visualization
Using Imagery and Imagination for Self-Transformation
New York: Destiny Books, 1998

Smith, C. Michael

Jung and Shamanism in Dialogue
London: Trafford Publishing, 2007

Spiller, Jan

Astrology for the Soul
New York: Bantam, 1997

Stone, Hal & Stone, Sidra

Embracing Our Selves
The Voice Dialogue Manual
San Rafael, CA: New World Library, 1989

Du bist viele
Das 100fache Selbst und seine Entdeckung durch
die Voice-Dialogue Methode
München: Heyne Verlag, 1994

Thorsson, Edred

Futhark
A Handbook of Rune Magic
San Francisco: Weiser Books, 1984

Tolle, Eckhart

The Power of Now
A Guide to Spiritual Enlightenment
Novato, CA: New World Library, 2004

Jetzt! Die Kraft der Gegenwart
Ein Leitfaden zum spirituellen Erwachen
Bielefeld: Kamphausen Verlag, 2000

A New Earth
Awakening to Your Life's Purpose
New York: Michael Joseph (Penguin), 2005

Eine neue Erde
Bewusstseinssprung anstelle von Selbstzerstörung
München: Goldmann, 2005

Too, Lillian

Feng Shui
Kuala Lumpur: Konsep Books, 1994

Villoldo, Alberto

Healing States
A Journey Into the World of Spiritual Healing and Shamanism
With Stanley Krippner
New York: Simon & Schuster (Fireside), 1987

Dance of the Four Winds
Secrets of the Inca Medicine Wheel
With Eric Jendresen
Rochester: Destiny Books, 1995

Die Macht der vier Winde
Eine Reise ins Reich der Schamanen
München: Goldmann, 2009

Shaman, Healer, Sage
How to Heal Yourself and Others with the Energy Medicine
of the Americas
New York: Harmony, 2000

Hüter des alten Wissens
Schamanisches Heilen im Medizinrad
Darmstadt: Schirner Verlag, 2007

Healing the Luminous Body
The Way of the Shaman with Dr. Alberto Villoldo
DVD, Sacred Mysteries Productions, 2004

Mending The Past And Healing The Future with Soul Retrieval
New York: Hay House, 2005

Seelenrückholung: die Vergangenheit schamanistisch erkunden
Die Zukunft heilen
München, Goldmann, 2006

Wild, Leon D.

The Runes Workbook
A Step-by-Step Guide to Learning the Wisdom of the Staves
San Diego: Thunder Bay Press, 2004

Wilhelm, Helmut

The Wilhelm Lectures on the Book of Changes
Princeton: Princeton University Press, 1995

Wilhelm, Richard

The I Ching or Book of Changes
With C. Baynes
3rd Edition, Bollingen Series XIX
Princeton, NJ: Princeton University Press, 1967

Williams, Strephon Kaplan

Dreams and Spiritual Growth
With Patricia H. Berne and Louis M. Savary
New York: Paulist Press, 1984

Durch Traumarbeit zum eigenen Selbst
Die Jung-Senoi Methode
Interlaken: Ansata Verlag, 1987

Dream Cards
Understand Your Dreams and Enrich Your Life
New York: Simon & Schuster (Fireside), 1991

Wing, R. L.

The I Ching Workbook
Garden City, N.Y.: Doubleday, 1984

Das Arbeitsbuch zum I Ching
Mit Chinesischen Orakel Münzen
München: Goldmann, 2004

Het I Tjing Werkboek
Baarn: Bigot & Van Rossum, 1986

Wolf, Fred Alan

Taking the Quantum Leap
The New Physics for Nonscientists
New York: Harper & Row, 1989

Der Quantensprung ist keine Hexerei
Frankfurt/M: Fischer Verlag, 1990

Parallel Universes
New York: Simon & Schuster, 1990

The Dreaming Universe
A Mind-Expanding Journey into the Realm
Where Psyche and Physics Meet
New York: Touchstone, 1995

The Eagle's Quest
A Physicist Finds the Scientific Truth At the Heart of the Shamanic World
New York: Touchstone, 1997

Die Physik der Träume
Frankfurt/M: DTV Verlag, 1997

Mind into Matter
A New Alchemy of Science and Spirit
New York: Moment Point Press, 2000

Wydra, Nancilee

Feng Shui
The Book of Cures
Lincolnwood: Contemporary Books, 1996

MYTHOLOGY QUOTES

by Joseph Campbell

"If you do follow your bliss you put yourself on a kind of track that has been there all the while, waiting for you, and the life that you ought to be living is the one you are living. Follow your bliss and don't be afraid, and doors will open where you didn't know they were going to be."

"Myth is much more important and true than history. History is just journalism and you know how reliable that is."

"Is the system going to flatten you out and deny you your humanity, or are you going to be able to make use of the system to the attainment of human purposes?"

"Myth must be kept alive. The people who can keep it alive are the artists of one kind or another."

"Myths are public dreams, dreams are private myths.

"We must be willing to get rid of the life we planned, so as to have the life that is waiting for us."

"I have bought this wonderful machine — a computer ... it seems to me to be an Old Testament god, with a lot of rules and no mercy."

— Joseph Campbell

FROM THE SAME AUTHOR

A Bibliography

You can search publications from here:
http://ipublica.com/books/

For audio books and music, you can start here:
http://ipublica.com/audio/

All paperbacks, audio downloads, audio book compact discs, music downloads and music compact discs, as well as Kindle books, are referenced on the site.

For free podcasts search iTunes under my author name.

For quoting my publications, please use the following form:
Pierre F. Walter, [Title]: [Subtitle], Newark: Sirius-C Media Galaxy LLC, 2011

Web Presence

Pierre F. Walter on the Web

Sites

http://authoryourlife.com

http://ipublica.com

http://ipublica.net

http://ipublica.org

http://ipublica.tv

Video Channels

http://youtube.com/user/ipublica

http://youtube.com/user/authoryourlife

http://vimeo.com/pierrefwalter/channels

http://ipublica.blip.tv/

http://authoryourlife.blip.tv/

http://emosexuality.blip.tv/

http://pierrefwalter.blip.tv/